Little Jamie Book

What It's Like to Be...
Qué se siente al ser...

MARIANO RIVERA

BY/POR
JOHN BANKSTON

TRANSLATED BY/
TRADUCIDO POR
EIDA DE LA VEGA

Mitchell Lane

P.O. Box 196
Hockessin, Delaware 19707
Visit us on the web: www.mitchelllane.com
Comments? Email us:
mitchelllane@mitchelllane.com

Mitchell Lane

PUBLISHERS

Printing   1   2   3   4   5   6   7   8   9

A LITTLE JAMIE BOOK

What It's Like to Be . . .	Qué se siente al ser . . .
América Ferrera	América Ferrera
Cameron Díaz	Cameron Díaz
George López	George López
Jennifer López	Jennifer López
The Jonas Brothers	Los Hermanos Jonas
Kaká	Kaká
Mariano Rivera	Mariano Rivera
Mark Sánchez	Mark Sánchez
Marta Vieira	Marta Vieira
Miley Cyrus	Miley Cyrus
Óscar De La Hoya	Óscar De La Hoya
Pelé	Pelé
President Barack Obama	El presidente Barack Obama
Ryan Howard	Ryan Howard
Selena Gómez	Selena Gómez
Shakira	Shakira
Sonia Sotomayor	Sonia Sotomayor
Vladimir Guerrero	Vladimir Guerrero

Library of Congress Cataloging-in-Publication Data
Bankston, John, 1974–
  What it's like to be Mariano Rivera / by John Bankston ; translated by Eida de la Vega = Qué se siente al ser Mariano Rivera / por John Bankston ; traducido por Eida de la Vega.
    p. cm. — (A little jamie book / un libro "little jamie")
  Includes bibliographical references and index.
  ISBN 978-1-61228-320-3 (library bound)
1. Rivera, Mariano, 1969– —Juvenile literature. 2. Baseball players—Panama—Biography—Juvenile literature. I. Vega, Eida de la. II. Title. III. Title: Qué se siente al ser Mariano Rivera.
  GV865.R496B36 2012
  796.357092 — dc23
  [B]
                                                                                    2012028101
eBook ISBN: 9781612283906

What It's Like to Be... /
Qué se siente al ser...

MARIANO
RIVERA

Mariano Rivera is best known as a baseball player for the New York Yankees. He is also called "Mo."

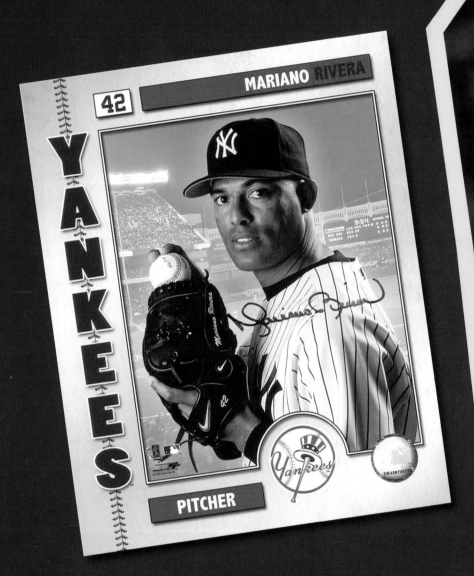

Mariano Rivera es un conocido jugador de béisbol de los Yankees de Nueva York. También le dicen "'Mo".

Pitcher/
Lanzador

Mariano was born on November 29, 1969 in Panama City, Panama. Panama is a country in Central America that is more than 1,000 miles south of Miami, Florida. Mariano says that the village where he grew up, named Puerto Caimito, is a very poor town. Mariano has one older sister, and two younger brothers.

Mariano nació el 29 de noviembre de 1969 en Ciudad Panamá, Panamá. Panamá es un país de América Central que está a más de 1000 millas al sur de Miami, Florida. Mariano dice que el pueblo donde creció, llamado Puerto Caimito, es un pueblo muy pobre. Mariano tiene una hermana mayor y dos hermanos menores.

Although Mariano played baseball and soccer, he liked soccer better. When he and his friends played baseball, they used cardboard boxes to make gloves. They used tree branches for bats and played with pink rubber balls. Mariano's father bought him his first real baseball mitt when he was twelve.

Aunque Mariano jugaba béisbol y fútbol, le gustaba más el fútbol. Cuando sus amigos y él jugaban béisbol, usaban cajas de cartón para hacer guantes. Usaban ramas de árboles como bates y jugaban con pelotas de goma rosadas. El padre de Mariano le compró su primer guante de béisbol de verdad cuando tenía doce años.

Mariano and his son Jaziel in the outfield during batting practice.

Mariano y su hijo Jaziel en los jardines durante la práctica de bateo.

Jaziel

Mariano dreamed of being paid to be a professional soccer player. But after he hurt his ankle playing soccer at Pedro Pablo Sánchez High School, he could not run very well. Instead of playing soccer, Mariano went to work for his dad catching sardines. Mariano was sixteen years old and it was very hard work. He knew he didn't want to spend his life catching tiny fish.

Sardines/
Sardinas

Mariano soñaba con que le pagaran por ser jugador de fútbol profesional. Pero después de lesionarse el tobillo jugando fútbol en la escuela secundaria Pedro Pablo Sánchez, no podía correr muy bien. En vez de jugar fútbol, Mariano fue a trabajar con su papá pescando sardinas. Mariano tenía dieciséis años y era un trabajo muy duro. Sabía que no quería pasarse toda la vida atrapando pececitos diminutos.

Father/
Padre

Mariano

IYOEL

For fun, Mariano began playing baseball for a local team called Panamá Oeste. He played shortstop, the person who stands between second and third base. It is a very difficult position to play because more balls go to the shortstop than anywhere else. Mariano was not very good.

Para divertirse, Mariano empezó a jugar béisbol en un equipo local llamado Panamá Oeste. Jugaba como torpedero, la persona que se para entre segunda y tercera bases. Es una posición muy difícil de jugar porque es a donde se dirigen las pelotas con más frecuencia. Mariano no era muy bueno.

Outfielder/ *Jardinero*

Shortstop/ *Torpedero*

Third baseman/ *Tercera base*

Pitcher/ *Lanzador*

Catcher/ *Receptor*

12

Baseball teams often send scouts all over the world to watch young baseball players. A scout's job is to find players who are good enough to be professionals. In 1987, a scout watched Mariano playing shortstop, but he didn't think Mariano was good enough.

Los equipos de béisbol envían con frecuencia cazadores de talentos por todo el mundo para observar a los jugadores de béisbol jóvenes. El trabajo de un cazador de talentos es encontrar jugadores lo suficientemente buenos para ser profesionales. En 1987, un cazador de talentos observó a Mariano jugando como torpedero, pero no pensó que era lo suficientemente bueno.

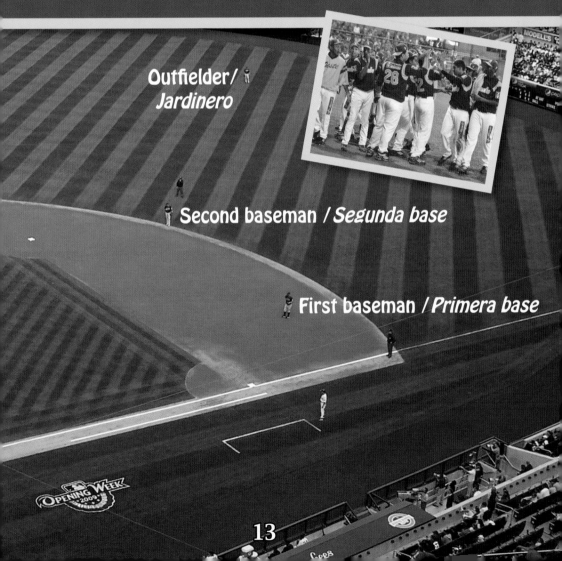

Outfielder/ *Jardinero*

Second baseman / *Segunda base*

First baseman / *Primera base*

The next year, Mariano asked if he could try pitching. Panamá Oeste's pitcher at the time wasn't playing very well. It turned out that Mariano was very good at throwing the ball. When the scout returned and saw him again, he asked Mariano to play for the New York Yankees!

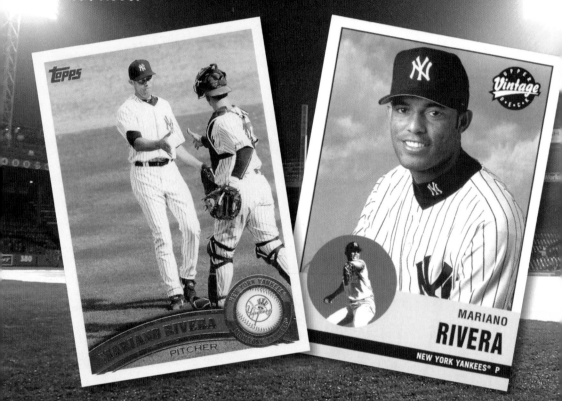

Al año siguiente, Mariano pidió que lo dejaran lanzar. El lanzador de Panamá Oeste en esa época no estaba jugando muy bien. Resultó que Mariano era muy bueno lanzando la pelota. Cuando el cazador de talentos regresó y lo volvió a observar, le pidió a Mariano que jugara ¡para los Yankees de Nueva York!

15

In 1990, Mariano began playing professional baseball. It was the first time he had ever left Panama. He did not speak English, and he was scared and homesick. He started out in the minor leagues, where he practiced and worked hard for five years.

				MARIANO RIVERA						**133**	

1 OF 500

MLB	CAREER					STATISTICS					
YR	TEAM	W	L	ERA	G	SV	IP	H	R	BB	K
'90	GC YANKEES	5	1	0.17	22	1	52	17	3	7	58
'91	GREENSB	4	9	2.75	29	0	114.2	102	48	36	123
'92	FT LAUD	5	3	2.28	10	0	59.1	40	17	5	42
'93	GREENSB	1	0	2.06	10	0	39.1	31	12	15	32
'93	GC YANKEES	0	1	2.25	2	0	4	2	1	1	6
'94	TAMPA	3	0	2.21	7	0	36.2	34	12	12	27
'94	ALB-COL	3	0	2.27	9	0	63.1	58	20	8	39
'94	COLUMBUS	4	2	5.81	6	0	31	34	22	10	23
'95	COLUMBUS	2	2	2.10	7	0	30	25	10	3	30
'95	YANKEES	5	3	5.51	19	0	67	71	43	30	51
'96	YANKEES	8	3	2.09	61	5	107.2	73	25	34	130
TOTALS		13	6	3.40	80	5	174.2	144	68	64	181

HEIGHT: 6'4"

WEIGHT: 168

BATS: RIGHT

THROWS: RIGHT

BORN: 11/29/69

En 1990, Mariano empezó a jugar béisbol profesional. Era la primera vez que viajaba fuera de Panamá. No hablaba inglés, tenía miedo y extrañaba su país. Empezó en las ligas menores, donde practicó y trabajó duro durante cinco años.

17

After he started playing professionally, Mariano married Clara Younce in 1991. Mariano and Clara had met many years before, in elementary school. They later had three sons, named Mariano Jr., Jafet, and Jaziel.

Mariano Jr.

Clara

Después de empezar a jugar profesionalmente, Mariano se casó con Clara Younce en 1991. Mariano y Clara se habían conocido muchos años atrás en la escuela primaria. Más tarde tuvieron tres hijos llamados Mariano Jr., Jafet y Jaziel.

Jafet

Jaziel

Manager/
Director
Joe Torre

189
BATS: R
THROWS: R
HEIGHT: 6'4"
WEIGHT: 168
BORN:
11/29/69

ROOKIE

MARIANO RIVERA   P

A tall control pitcher with a 90-mph fastball, Mariano made 10
starts during the Yankees' successful wild-card bid. He later pro-
vided solid relief in the Division Series against Seattle.

YEAR	TEAM	W	L	ERA	G	CG	IP	H	BB	K	BSRN	DAA
1995	YANKEES	5	3	5.51	19	0	67	71	43	30	51	13.8	.266
CAREER TOTALS		5	3	5.51	19	0	67	71	43	30	51	13.8	.266

In May of 1995, Mariano learned he would play Major League Baseball for the first time. When he found out, he was in a hotel room, and he was so happy that he jumped up and down on his bed!

En mayo de 1995, Mariano se enteró de que iba a jugar en las Ligas Mayores de Béisbol por primera vez. Cuando se enteró, estaba en una habitación de hotel y se puso tan contento ¡que empezó a saltar en la cama!

Once he went to the Major League, Mariano Rivera became a special kind of pitcher, called a closer. His job was to pitch near the end of the game. If his team was ahead and he kept them ahead, he "saved" the game. Mariano has saved more games than any other pitcher in the history of Major League Baseball. He does this with a special kind of pitch that is very hard to hit, called a cutter. Most pitchers throw all kinds of pitches, but almost every pitch Mariano throws is a cutter.

Cuando entró en las Ligas Mayores, Mariano se convirtió en un tipo de lanzador especial, llamado cerrador. Su trabajo era lanzar casi al final del juego. Si su equipo llevaba ventaja y él lo mantenía adelante, "salvaba" el juego. Mariano ha salvado más juegos que cualquier otro lanzador en la historia de las Ligas Mayores de béisbol. Hace esto con un lanzamiento muy especial que es muy difícil de batear, llamado "cutter". La mayoría de los lanzadores tienen muchos tipos de lanzamientos, pero casi cada lanzamiento de Mariano es un "cutter".

Cutter

Andy Pettitte

Derek Jeter

Jorge Posada

24

The winner of the World Series is considered the best team in baseball. The year after Mariano began playing for the Yankees, they won their first World Series in eighteen years! After the 1996 win, he helped them to win four more: in 1998, 1999, 2000, and 2009.

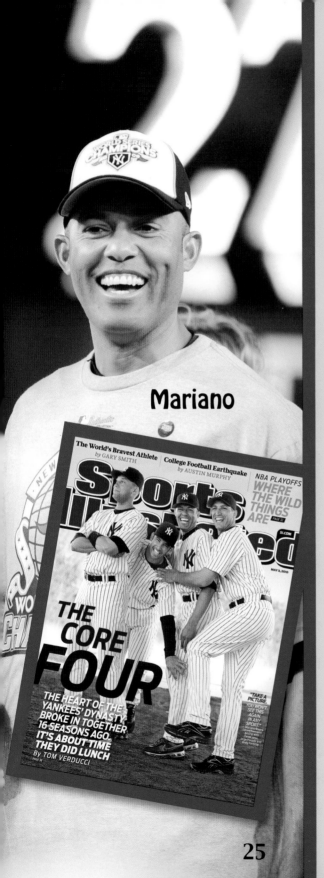

Mariano

El ganador de la Serie Mundial es considerado el mejor equipo de béisbol. Al año siguiente de que Mariano empezara a jugar con ellos, ¡los Yankees ganaron su primera Serie Mundial luego de dieciocho años! Después del triunfo de 1996, él los ayudó a ganar cuatro más: en 1998, 1999, 2000 y 2009.

Mariano with kids from Tuesday's Children, a program to benefit children who lost their parents in the 9/11 terrorist attack.

Mariano has become a very successful baseball player, and he is paid a lot of money. It is very important to Mariano to use his money to help other people. He started a foundation that helps children in villages like the one he grew up in. The foundation provides people with food, health care, and education. He says he wants to make sure that talented kids have a chance to learn more and share their talents with others.

Mariano con niños de Tuesday's Children, un programa que beneficia a niños que perdieron a sus padres en el ataque terrorista del 11 de septiembre.

Mariano se ha convertido en un jugador de béisbol con mucho éxito, y le pagan mucho dinero. Es muy importante para Mariano usar su dinero para ayudar a otras personas. Fundó una organización que ayuda a niños de pueblos parecidos a donde él se crió. La fundación le da alimentos, cuidados médicos y educación a la gente. Él dice que se quiere asegurar de que los niños con talento tengan una oportunidad de aprender más y compartir sus talentos con otros.

In 2012, at forty-two years old, Mariano said he would only play for one more season. Although he is older than most professional baseball players, he continues to "save" games for the Yankees. Even after he finally retires, Mariano will be known to many as one of the greatest pitchers of all time.

En el 2012, a los cuarenta y dos años de edad, Mariano dijo que sólo jugaría una temporada más. Aunque él es mayor que la mayoría de los jugadores de béisbol profesionales, continúa "salvando" juegos de los Yankees. Incluso, si finalmente se retira, Mariano será recordado por muchos como uno de los grandes lanzadores de todos los tiempos.

Levin, Judith. *Mariano Rivera*. New York: Infobase Publishing, 2009.

Manning, Sean. *Top of the Order: 25 Writers Pick Their Favorite Baseball Player of All Time*. Cambridge, MA: Da Capo Press, 2010.

Pietrusza, David. *The New York Yankees Baseball Team*. Springfield, NJ: Enslow Publishers, 1998.

Rappoport, Ken. *Baseball's Top 10 Pitchers*. Berkeley Heights, NJ: Enslow Publishers, 2011.

Sherman, Joel, and David Cone. *Birth of a Dynasty: Behind the Pinstripes with the 1996 Yankees*. Emmaus, PA: Rodale, 2006.

INTERNET SITES/
SITIOS DE INTERNET

The Mariano Rivera Foundation, http://themarianoriverafoundation.org/

New York Yankees Official Web Site, http://newyork.yankees.mlb.com/team/player.jsp?player_id=121250

Pitching Tips - How to Throw the Cutter, http://www.thecompletepitcher.com/how_to_throw_cutter.htm

Sports Illustrated, http://sportsillustrated.cnn.com/vault

WORKS CONSULTED/
OBRAS CONSULTADAS

Castillo, Luis, and William Cane. *Clubhouse Confidential: A Yankee Bat Boy's Insider Tale*. New York: St. Martin's Press, 2011.

"Chatter box," *The New York Times*, September 25, 2011.

Gere, Richard. "Richard Gere Interviews Mariano Rivera." Gotham, April/May 2012.

Hermoso, Rafael. "Where Rivera Goes For Relief Takes Hat Off To Panama." *New York Daily News*, August 31, 1998.

Hille, Bob. "Mariano Rivera and his Fastball are a Cut Above," *The Sporting News*, November 1, 1999.

Red, Christian. "Modern Yankee Heroes: From Humble Beginnings" *New York Daily News*, March 13, 2010. http://articles.nydailynews.com/2010-03-13/sports/27058930_1_puerto-caimito-cardboard-cousin

Rosen, Charley. *Bullpen Diaries: Mariano Rivera, Bronx Dreams, Pinstripe Legends and the Future of the New York Yankees*. New York: Harper, 2011.

Stottlemyre, Mel, and John Harper. *Pride and Pinstripes: The Yankees, Mets, and Surviving Life's Challenges*. New York: HarperEntertainment, 2007.

Verducci, Tom. "So Far, So Good." *Sports Illustrated*, May 3, 2010. http://sportsillustrated.cnn.com/vault/article/magazine/MAG1168943/index.htm

Verducci, Tom. "The Sure Thing." *Sports Illustrated*, November 11, 2009. http://sportsillustrated.cnn.com/vault/article/magazine/MAG1162903/index.htm

Waldstein, David. "Rivera Hints This Is His Last Yankees Season." *The New York Times*. February 20, 2012.

Wendel, Tim, and Bob Costas. *The New Face of Baseball: The One-Hundred Year Rise and Triumph of Latinos in America's Favorite Sport*. New York: Rayo, 2003.

PHOTO CREDITS: Cover, p. 3—Nick Laham/Getty Images; p. 5—Patrick McDermott/Getty Images; p. 7—Linda Cataffo/NY Daily News Archive via Getty Images; p. 9, 24–25—Corey Spikin/NY Dail News Archive via Getty Images; pp. 10–11—Ronald C. Modra/Sports Imagery/Getty Images; pp. 14–15, 22–23—Al Bello/Getty Images; pp. 22, 23, 25, 28—Walter Iooss Jr./Sports Illustrated/Getty Images; p. 17—Peter Muhly/AFP/Getty Images; pp. 18–19—Jared Wickerham/Getty Images; pp. 20–21—Peter Muhly/AFP/Getty Images; pp. 26–27, 28–29—AP Photo/Kathy Kmonicek; p. 30—Reuters/Mike Segar. Every effort has been made to locate all copyright holders of materials used in this book. Any errors or omissions will be corrected in future editions of the book.

INDEX/ÍNDICE

ABOUT THE AUTHOR: Born in Boston, Massachusetts, John Bankston began writing articles while still a teenager. Since then, over two hundred of his articles have been published in magazines and newspapers across the country, including travel articles in *The Tallahassee Democrat*, *The Orlando Sentinel*, and *The Tallahassean*. He is the author of over sixty biographies for young adults, including works on Drew Barrymore, Jessica Simpson, and Mandy Moore. One of his fondest memories is riding the "T" with his father and watching the Red Sox play in Fenway Park. He currently lives in Newport Beach, California.

ACERCA DEL AUTOR: Nacido en Boston, Massachusetts, John Bankston empezó a escribir artículos de adolescente. Desde entonces, ha publicado más de 200 artículos en revistas y periódicos de todo el país, incluyendo artículos de viajes en *The Tallahassee Democrat*, *The Orlando Sentinel* y *The Tallahassean*. Es autor de más de sesenta biografías para jóvenes, que incluyen trabajos sobre Drew Barrymore, Jessica Simpson, y Mandy Moore. Uno de sus recuerdos más preciados es montar el metro de Boston con su papá y ver jugar a los Medias Rojas en el Fenway Park. Actualmente vive en Newport Beach, California.

ABOUT THE TRANSLATOR: Eida de la Vega was born in Havana, Cuba, and now lives in New Jersey with her mother, her husband, and her two children. Eida has worked at Lectorum/ Scholastic, and as editor of the magazine *Selecciones del Reader's Digest*.

ACERCA DE LA TRADUCTORA: Eida de la Vega nació en La Habana, Cuba, y ahora vive en Nueva Jersey con su madre, su esposo y sus dos hijos. Ha trabajado en Lectorum/Scholastic y, como editora, en la revista *Selecciones del Reader's Digest*.